TILT

Works by Vincentia Schroeter

Communication Breakthrough, How Using Brain Science and Listening to Body Cues Can Transform Your Relationships.
Schroeter, V., Wolfheart Press (2018).
Available at Amazon or website:
www.vincentiaschroeterphd.com

Bend Into Shape, Techniques for Bioenergetic Therapists. Schroeter, V. and Thomson, B. LLPrinters (USA); Psycho-Sozial Verlag (in English; in Spanish as *Dando Forma*). Franco-Angeli (in Italian as *Il Se' Cerca Il Corpo*) (2011).

"Wall Between Oneself and the World". Revelation of the Breath - its Power, Wisdom and Beauty. Ed. Sharon Mijares, Suny Books, New York (2009).

TILT

*Seeking Balance in
Troubled Times*

Vincentia Schroeter

I dedicate this book to my two young grandsons, who live five states away from me. Because of the pandemic, it broke my heart not to see them in person in 2020. I love playing soccer with Hayden and playing dinosaurs with Harrison. I miss following both of you into your worlds. You light up my life.

Contents

Introduction

2020 has felt like riding in a little boat rocking on choppy seas in storms that keep coming. If like me, you don't have the sailing skills of Moana (and she had divine help), you have been in for a rough ride. I see you. The stormy skies of 2020, including a pandemic, along with economic, climate and political strain, have created a feeling of ongoing trauma. Many of us struggle with anxiety, depression, anger, fear, and loneliness in all this turmoil. When the sea never calms, it is as if we need to be on alert all the time, which is exhausting. Always being on the lookout depletes us, making it hard to find peace and joy.

How are you holding up? Is it harder to sleep, harder to focus, harder to be patient, harder to avoid another piece of unneeded chocolate? I know that is one comfort I go toward when I want to escape.

My mission is to help you see that feeling anxious, overeating, having trouble sleeping, and being short-tempered are normal responses. Our moods are a reaction to a world off-kilter. They are our attempt to create some sense of safety or protection when we feel ungrounded. We are doing the best we can, and it makes sense that we are suffering.

I have been a psychotherapist for over forty years. I have a specialty in Bioenergetic Analysis, which works with chronic tension patterns in the body to help transform developmental and acute trauma. In my work, I apply the latest understanding in neuroscience of how the brain affects mood. In addition to seeing our current suffering in these unprecedented times as expected, I also want to promote some healthy coping skills, the kinds that do not cause you to fall overboard, drowning in emotional or physical hangovers.

This book is presented in chronological order, starting from the first month of the pandemic. It captures ways in which we tried to navigate these rough seas. In some chapters I offer my thoughts; in others I pair the story with concrete coping tools.

My goal is to help you see this turbulent time with new eyes, feel some compassion, and perhaps some grace for yourself and others. I invite you to flip through this book and look for a sliver of hope, a glimpse of gold breaking through the dark grey clouds.

Tilt

March 13, 2020:
Day one of shelter-in-place order

Astay-at-home order has just been issued in the USA and most of us are in shock. The Coronavirus is like a fast-moving wind gaining strength as it sweeps through America from across the sea. We batten down the hatches and take shelter from the storm to try and keep the invaders out. Testing supplies are sparse; treatment teams for the infected are strained. While the virus is lifting in China, where it was first discovered on December 31, 2019, it is still sweeping through the rest of the world, and a vaccine may take a year to develop.

This pandemic is causing stress, strain, and panic around the world. Last night I pictured the globe tilting on a pinpoint and twirling precariously. The ground beneath my feet felt slippery.

I heard loud rain. I looked up and saw arrows shoot down from the sky and bounce white dots against the red brick stones outside. The sky seemed to be angry and the earth was saying, "Don't come out here, it isn't safe." How do we cope when we feel this kind of sudden upending of our lives? Here are some comments I recently heard from family and neighbors.

How do I manage my anxiety?

If I don't work, I don't get paid.

How do I move through this without going crazy?

I feel inundated with the bad news that changes daily.

My neighbors are in denial and are carrying on as usual. I'm so mad at them.

I don't want to be confined at home.

Relax, you are overreacting.

I faced long lines at the store and there was no toilet paper left. I want this to be over.

WHAT CAN WE DO?

All of these sentiments are to be expected in a world that changed overnight. How can we cope with this sudden somersault, this "new normal"?

The "new normal" of living in a pandemic has made us all feel very distressed. I have noticed the people around me reacting in a variety of ways. Some have refused to adjust their everyday activities, some are reacting a little slowly due to their shock, and some are in full lockdown or panic mode. These are normal reactions of our nervous system.

As a psychotherapist, I work with the concepts of the red, blue and green zones to help people understand and manage their emotional states. These mind states function differently under normal conditions and under stress.

The RED zone of our nervous system controls our fight/flight response. This can be a problem when we focus only on anger at others or are overreacting in fear. Both of these states compromise our immune system, which makes us more susceptible to illness.

The BLUE zone controls resting and digesting. But under stress the blue zone can make the body freeze in shock, sink into depression, or space out in denial, acting like nothing abnormal is happening. The human body is not meant to linger in these states as it strains our hearts and our well-being.

The GREEN zone is the part of the nervous system where we feel both calm and engaged. We think the most clearly and behave the most reasonably. In this state, we are open to seeing the pain in others and caring for our own. How can we steady ourselves when we feel off-balance?

How do we respond without excessive anger, fear, depression, or denial?

Here are some ways.

GETTING INTO THE GREEN ZONE

1. Use Your Breath to Get Centered

    Sit comfortably, close your eyes, and focus on your breath as it rises and falls. Next, try to slow your breath and deepen the inhale and exhale. Notice any sensations or feelings you have. Breathe into any areas of pain or tension in the body. Focusing on the sensation of breathing can help lower our anxiety or bring us energy when we are down.

For example, I just worked with someone who said she wanted to go from feeling "panicked to prudent". She closed her eyes, breathed slowly, and followed her sensations. After some tears and loosening of tension, she said, "I hear this voice inside say, 'It's going to be alright. We'll get through this.'" She opened her eyes with a new calmness about her. Then she said, "I need to remember this voice, when the scared voice wants to take over." Breathing and centering like this can lead you to a calmer state.

2. Help Others

Look outside yourself, open your heart, and think about some way you might aid someone else or contribute to a worthy cause. I recently saw this on my neighborhood website. A woman wrote, "I am a young, healthy gal; contact me and I can go get groceries for you."

3. Limit News to Stay Balanced

Stay informed but limit your daily dosage of news and use healthy distractions to stay balanced. Healthy distractions include activities or entertainment that intrigue you, such as sports, gardening, baking, computer games, or art.

4. Use Humor

Comedy can help to loosen your body and feed your spirit. I checked an app that I am on with my eleven siblings. One of my sisters sent a picture of earrings that look like toilet paper rolls. The caption read, "Commemorative jewelry to always remember 2020." Another sister shared this: "My cat just came home with twenty-four bags of kitty litter. When will this nonsense stop?" I viewed a video of two of my brothers doing a flamenco type dance to a new tune, "corona-veerus", as they cleared out an office. I laughed and felt my stress level go down immediately.

As this storm rages and throws us off balance, we can look for ways like these to feel more grounded on this tilted planet. My wish for you is that you will feel the ground as solid beneath your feet as you walk through these next few weeks in a world that is trying to cope.

Couples and COVID-19

March 20, 2020:
Week two of shelter-in-place order

Ten thousand people have died from COVID-19 worldwide. We have been in stay-at-home lockdown for one week in the USA and are still reeling as we try to adjust to dramatic changes in our everyday lives. While it is still early in the crisis, couples are already being impacted.

Being in such close quarters day after day can lead to conflicts and unique challenges. How can couples navigate the new normal of being in each other's company 24/7 in these days of forced confinement? My sister knows a man who was dating a woman for only two weeks when they went away for a weekend to the mountains. The woman became ill and the man had to take her to the emergency room twice. Then the shelter-in-place command came, and they are now stuck together in the mountains and barely know each other. Other couples have been together for years but have created wide circles, even within their homes, to keep a distance and sometimes to avoid intimacy. For most couples, being in each other's space all the time is new, and while it creates opportunities for closeness, it can also cause stress.

There are extra strains put on couples due to the global pandemic. Some of these strains are the constant vigilance to avoid illness, the grief of lost lives, the anger some feel at those who ignore shelter-in-place laws, and sadness at missing loved ones we cannot touch. We worry about money and supplies and may feel anger at authorities slow to make the planet's health their primary directive. Political strife abounds, as does concern for medical professionals and others on the front line of this war against the virus.

What can help couples manage these days, weeks, and likely months of being stuck at home together? Here are some suggestions.

1. Create a Schedule

   Choose a schedule that organizes your day to include a balance between closeness, personal space, work and play.

2. Consider Bringing in Outside Help

   Couples counseling or a support group, both widely available online through tele-psychology, can be an immense aid.

3. Learn Some New Communication Tools

Improve your ability to convey your thoughts and ideas to your partner. Say you feel some conflict with your partner but do not know how to discuss it. One powerful tool for clear communication is using a whole message. You can read more about this technique in my book, *Communication Breakthrough, How Using Brain Science and Listening to Body Cues Can Transform Your Relationships.*

Tell your partner the following four parts in this order:

1. the facts of the situation ("...happened and then...happened")
2. what you think or your values ("I believe that...")
3. how you feel - your emotions, such as angry, sad, hurt, glad, or scared ("I feel...)
4. what you want or need, such as ("I want to go into couples counseling")

This one tool can improve the experience of living in close contact with a partner for more extended periods than usual.

4. Give a Compliment

When someone in my family has a birthday, I may send them a message via email or text, or snail mail that includes a compliment about their unique qualities or what I appreciate about them. On my niece's thirty-second birthday, I wrote, "You are on fire with your career. You are a bright, compassionate wonder woman! Enjoy your day." Compliments fit in all settings. If you look around, you can usually find a way to compliment a co-worker (on a job well done?), a friend (maybe their kindness or patience?), a child (did a chore without being prodded?), or a partner/spouse (their looks today? their way of acting loving?).

5. Ask About Their Day

I do not like to ask a child or working adult in my family, "How was your day?" because they are often likely to say, "Fine". End of conversation. Just to hold their attention a bit longer, I ask, "What happened at work today?" This makes them dig deeper. I might ask a school-age child, "What was the best (or worst) part of your day?" This way, if they want to debrief their day, I am there to listen. This often helps them let go of their "work" day and feel lighter. You can ask a friend or your co-worker about their previous evening or recent events in their life.

6. Be Verbally or Physically Affectionate

Physical contact in this time of the pandemic is restricted to those we live with or have decided to let into our orbit of safety. This results in a shortage of the love hormones that often pass between human beings with physical touch. Physical isolation increases stress. But there was a time and there will be time again for more physical contact.

When we were kids, we would huddle together on the carpet in our living room to watch TV or play games. Wrestling play was called "mauling". Once we got tired, we leaned into each other on the carpet or couch to rest. Our parents called this "the puppy pile". After my mother's funeral ten years ago, many of us, though full-grown adults, grabbed sleeping bags and slept all piled together in that same living room to soak up our grief in each other's familiar warmth.

Physical affection varies in what is appropriate in each family, each setting, and each relationship. We are most spontaneous with those we feel safest being around. If you are not prone to be affectionate, try something easy like a pat on the shoulder. Take a breath and focus on the other person. If they seem to be receiving your affection, good. They will feel more positive and so will you. Verbal affection is any kind of statement from the heart, such as, "I like you" or "I love you". This even works over video chat across the miles.

7. Give a Surprise

When one of my sisters shows up at my house, she will come bearing gifts and hand out little presents that she got here and there from her travels. My husband Steve came home from work with a surprise gift for me, a *LIFE* magazine special edition, "Paul at 75". A whole issue about my favorite Beatle! Yeah! I remember looking at my husband as I held it to my chest and took a breath. We are still here. Healthy for now. Love fills my heart and I cherish his presence.

Inside

April 2020:
Month two of quarantine

One hundred thousand people have died from COVID-19 worldwide, and we are well into our second month of quarantine in California and much of the USA. My husband and I are older, which puts us in the higher risk category for contracting the disease, so we follow the guidelines to stay home. Our food delivery routine is now working smoothly, as we get eggs from the chicken lady and vegetables from the farm, both delivered by kind neighbors. My younger sister delivers our other groceries. But I cannot hug her when she comes to the door. I feel sad watching her walk away. Once I close the door, we are inside the house, where most of us spend almost all our time.

The US just passed the twenty thousand mark in the number of Coronavirus deaths. Most citizens are doing a good job sheltering at home, which lowers the contagion rate of the virus. People are revealing their mental states in this time of crisis. Here are a few examples of sentiments I heard recently.

I am an anxious mess. I am exhausted. I can barely focus on work. I feel drained.

I want to call her, but I feel like I need her more than she needs me.

I hear a siren. Is a neighbor being hospitalized for the Coronavirus?

I feel like the walls of this apartment are closing in on me.

I just want to crawl under a blanket, but the kids are yelling for me.

Even in our safe houses, we know we are hiding from the big bad wolf, which we feel is waiting to pounce, maim, and kill. Those who must venture out are in stealth mode with all their personal protective equipment. Those more susceptible, like medical professionals, the homeless, prisoners, border detainees, delivery personnel, and anyone else interacting daily with strangers, are in more danger. People are out of work and scared about money. All of this increases stress.

Do you wonder how that affects your body? Let us take a peek inside.

This constant dark cloud over our heads, which is the fear of contracting a killer virus and the monumental task of combating it, puts us in what is called "survival mode". How does that state affect the brain and body? It keeps us on high alert, which raises our cortisol levels, making our bodies ready for fight or flight. Most of us have some history of trauma. When we were victims of trauma, we had no power to affect a horrifying or terrifying outcome. The current epic event can reactivate old traumas. It can make us feel a familiar powerlessness we felt in the past. As a result, some people are short-tempered, acting out anger as a way to feel power by fighting. Others react through depression and immobility. Both responses are the body's way of attempting to reduce that feeling of overwhelm. These are the body's natural responses.

Here are some solutions to consider for attending to the emotions inside.

1. Release the Energy of Held-In Anger

   When you feel you will explode in anger, hike to the top of a hill where you can be alone and sing or scream your protest to God or the sky. Avoid the impulse to be destructive but do something expressive to channel your rage, like writing, playing music, or exercising.

2. Reach Out for Help

   When you are scared, depressed, or exhausted, you could use outside soothing. If you do not have a pet or person you are sheltering with, call up friends or family. We all have more time for each other. We all need each other.

3. Practice Self-Compassion

   Accept your changing moods, especially the ones that drag you down. For example, you can inhale slowly and say something like, "Of course I am feeling down. I am doing the best I can right now in a situation I do not feel control over." Take a break, breathe into your belly and relax. Send yourself some light. We need to be gentle, not only toward others during these difficult times but toward ourselves, including the states inside our heads and hearts.

Pillow

April 2020

In the last week of month two of this pandemic, the dog peed on my favorite pillow. I threw it in the wash but soon heard the washing machine buck loudly. I squeezed out the trapped water, but the pillow was so water-heavy that the worn fabric tore, exposing soppy grey-white goose feathers.

I am sure I may have loved another pillow or two in my life, but this one had been with me through so much. Here are some moments we shared.

My husband drove my brand-new car, and some drunk lady hit him behind, destroying my back bumper. I was so angry, I marched upstairs, pounded my pillow, and screamed bloody murder into it.

When my parents died, I buried myself in the soft folds of my pillow and cried forever.

When I had been sick, I could mold it to support my aching head or bones in just the right way.

When my toddler grandson jumped on my bed, I hit him with my pillow, and he fell over laughing.

Other pillows come to mind: The pink one my friend used to prop her body as she recovered from breast cancer surgery; the small plaid one sewn by an eight-year-old neighbor for my doggie's bed; the ones people drag through airports because they need to sleep on their own pillow no matter where they go; the full body pillow I gave a patient when she was dying so she could sleep more comfortably.

I threw my favorite pillow in the trash today. I am going to miss you. You were stained and worn, soft and pliable. You absorbed my anger, soaked up my tears, and cushioned my dreams. You gave me support, comfort, and security. Thank you for your service.

Flutter By

May 20, 2020:
Month three living in pandemic

By the third month of the pandemic, I joined my husband in listening to recorded guided meditations before bed, in order to fall asleep more easily. My husband scrolled through a series of meditations that he got from an app called "Ten Percent Happier," put together by Dan Harris. Each night we were taken on a new journey. One night, as we settled into bed, I heard the voice of Sharon Salzberg (a Mindfulness Meditation teacher) as she invited us to "think of yourself at a different age, younger or older than you are now and offer the sayings of loving-kindness".

I saw myself in the future, at age ninety, sitting on the carpeted stairs in my house, just like my mother-in-law did at that age. I held a blank sketchbook and pencil, just like she did, and looked out the window at the trees. Then I said the words that go with the meditation, "May I feel safe, feel happy, feel healthy. May I be at ease."

My mother-in-law liked to write rhyming poems and draw butterflies sitting on mushrooms. Like her, as long as I have a sketchpad and my imagination, I want to write and draw. As long as I am not too scared. As her dementia grew more severe, she became more anxious. If I am not too fearful or too sick, I see myself happy at ninety.

After doing this meditation practice, I realized that I had learned lessons from this quarantine to help me at ninety (if I am blessed to live that long). First, I struggled with accepting being dependent on other people, like neighbors who bring eggs and veggies and my sister, who shops for and delivers our groceries. Now, I accept and appreciate their kindness.

Next, I learned to embrace a narrower circumference, to move around inside a smaller circle. My house, my backyard, my neighborhood—only as far as the one, two or three miles that my daily walks take me. Then I learned to fill those smaller spaces in a fuller way, like a butterfly who lights on a mushroom and slowly flaps her wings to soak the sun into her every vein.

And just Be.

More Here.

More Now.

Not flitting from one yard to the next, always searching for a new flower.

I was a butterfly, quick to flutter by.

Now I sit on the stairs and soak in the sunlight coming through the window.

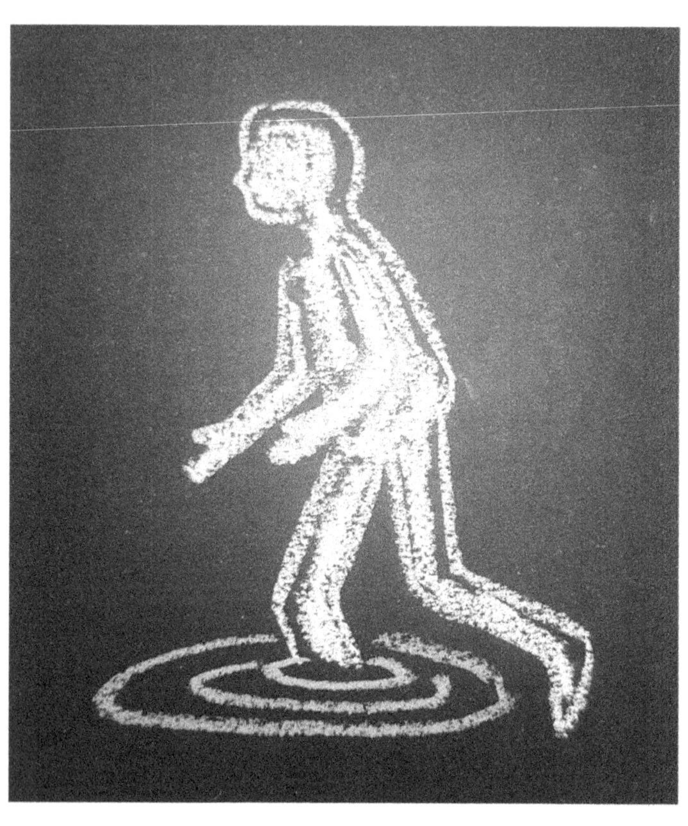

Conflict Quicksand

May 25, 2020:
Month three of pandemic

An article I read on Facebook during the third month of the pandemic noted that there was a marked increase in suicides in the USA since the COVID-19 quarantine started. The article concluded that the increasing suicide rate justifies ending shelter-in-place orders. This bothered me. As a psychotherapist, I am aware that suicidal impulses demand immediate action to save a life. Therapists say, "Suicide is a permanent solution to a temporary problem." This means that if you can intervene to treat the suicidal person when they are in danger, they often can stabilize. However, you cannot let the fear of the risks of loss of life in one form (suicide) make you throw caution to the wind for the other silent killer in our midst (COVID-19). I decided to respond to the woman who posted the article.

Here was how I responded to the article.

"This (the rising suicides) is distressing; however, it is not an either/or situation. An increase in suicides does not justify ending shelter-in-place… (I advocate for more mental health access) … We are dealing with death either way, suicide or Coronavirus… Both need to be tackled, one by safe distancing, one by access to mental health treatment."

I was a little taken aback by the responses back to me. Here are some of them.

"What about depression and suicide because of lost business?…therapy won't cure that… Please don't be so close-minded."

"…Also, SIP orders haven't proven that effective! God bless those trying to live their lives as they see fit. This is definitely an overreach!" (angry face emoji)

"…I could post lots of articles showing how shelter-in-place does not help much… If I talk of a devastated economy, I'll be accused of thinking money is more important than lives… What about the lives lost from the side effects of the economic shutdown? … Coronavirus…is not as deadly as first feared…look at the big picture…look at the real numbers."

Being called "close-minded" stung. I also noticed a common thread in the responses to me, statements like "Shelter-in-place orders are not very effective or do not help much"; "Coronavirus is not as deadly as first feared"; "Look at the real numbers…". The common thread is that these people do not believe the virus is very serious.

These opinions made me think that since these people believed the virus was not that bad, it made sense that they would be more focused on ending the (unuseful) shelter-in-place (SIP). If you believe the virus is not that bad, it makes sense your brain would look for and emphasize problems arising from SIP. This allowed me to understand their point of view better. Though I began to understand their perspective, I still disagreed with their opinion that I am "close-minded". I had no interest in staying in dialogue with these strangers on Facebook. But what if I was interested in keeping the conversation going? What if this was a roommate, family member, or co-worker who criticized me? What if I valued the relationship enough to try and stay in the arena and keep talking? This made me think about a technique for staying in contact when you feel unjustly criticized.

How can you stay in a dialogue when you feel unjustly criticized? Staying engaged without reacting from a place of anger or hurt can be difficult, but here is a technique you can use.

In Chapter 10 of my book *Communication Breakthrough*, I share three ways to stay open during conflict. This "Covering Technique" is one way to handle criticism. When falsely accused, you may feel angry and want to fight, or you may feel shame and want to shrink away. Covering helps you hang in there and keep the dialogue going. You can agree one of three ways: agree in part, in probability, or in principle. I want to apply the technique here in my case of being called "close-minded".

1. Agree in part: "Sometimes I can be close-minded…"

2. Agree in probability: "You may be right, I may be close-minded…"

3. Agree in principle: "It is true, if I believed that Coronavirus is not that deadly, and that quarantine

is causing more problems than it solves, I'd be close-minded to not be more open to ending SIP."

The Covering Technique's goal is to stay in the arena during conflict and continue the dialogue in a calm way. Why do this? It is a sign of resilience to be able to take criticism and keep listening. When you keep a contentious dialogue going, you may achieve some agreement or at least find some peace with your accuser.

In the case of my being criticized online, I do not have to respond to those posts from strangers and have decided not to because I am not involved personally with these people. You may also choose not to engage with strangers and may see it as a waste of your precious time.

However, I also see my post's responses as an example of a current, wide, ideological split in this society where what people see as "facts" varies based on what each wants to believe. When we cannot agree on what news is true and what is fake, it is hard to communicate effectively. It is like we are both standing on quicksand. Neither of us can get a foothold when the ground is not stable. Agreed upon facts create a solid foundation, which is in short supply in America these days. I feel sad about how divided we are as a nation and how little we seem to be able to reach across this divide.

Without that common belief in the same facts, what can we do?

Even if we cannot get our heads around the same facts, we can sense the feeling behind the opinions. Everyone seeks safety and security, and it is that need that is our common ground. People are sometimes afraid, worried and frustrated during this crisis. The more distress we feel, the less open-hearted we tend to be, and the more critical we are of others. When you feel unfairly criticized and want to keep the dialogue going, look for something to agree upon. This is at least one way to keep the door open.

Goats

May 31, 2020:
Final week of third month

Racial tensions exploded in violence in late May of 2020. This occurred amidst a background of people feeling confined and a mass loss of income due to the pandemic. There were proportionally more black than white deaths from COVID-19 in the USA. A video came out that Ahmad Aubrey, a black jogger, was killed by a white father and son who hopped out of their truck and shot and killed Aubrey. The perpetrators were only arrested when a video of the shooting emerged a month after the incident. The public became outraged.

Trevor Noah, the host of "The Daily Show", talked about the domino effect with recent racial tension in America[1]. Then the Amy Cooper video went viral and exposed the disparity between blacks and whites in relation to police in the USA. This woman, Amy Cooper, seeing the police as protective of her as a white person and hostile toward blacks, called 911 and said,

---

1   "George Floyd and the Dominoes of Racial Injustice." Trevor Noah, The Daily Social Distancing Show.

"An African-American man is threatening my life." The man, Chris Cooper, was just bird watching and had asked her to leash her dog as is the law in the park. He knew his life was put in peril by her call, and so did she. Watching Amy use her white privilege to endanger this man's life highlighted racial disparity and that, according to Noah, was "the first domino". Then came footage of George Floyd. He was pulled from his car, not resisting arrest, handcuffed, pushed to the ground, and held down by three cops. One cop kept his knee on Floyd's neck for over eight minutes, while Floyd said, "I can't breathe" and called out the names of those he loved. George Floyd died. The entire world reacted. This, said Noah, was "the second domino".

After Floyd's death, big cities in America burst into flames with protests against racial injustice. Scared business owners boarded up their stores. Trevor Noah said that people complained about looters but stated that the distress over this domino effect increased the outrage that contributed to violence. He made sense of it this way. While looking straight into the TV camera and leaning forward, Noah said, "The 'contract' we all sign as a society is made up of common rules that all agree on, like that police will be here to protect and serve all citizens. That contract is broken." He said, "You don't like Target being looted? Police in America are looting black bodies." Noah asked, "If the people at the top do not uphold the contract, what is it worth?"

Often spearheading looting and violence in cities are undercover white nationalists who travel from outside the area. Like a powder keg, once they instigate violence, like breaking a store window, angry others will join in.

Their agenda is to get the destruction blamed solely on angry black people so that society will not address the systemic racism in this country.

Here are reactions to the May 2020 violence from some of my family members.

From my sister in Sacramento: "We were watching Netflix and smelled smoke, heard the choppers and knew it was getting closer. I watched live broadcasts of hundreds of police in riot gear on J Street firing shots into protestors to disperse them. It only made them madder. It was like the sixties/seventies. I was so disturbed; I couldn't go to sleep until two in the morning. It's not supposed to be like this!"

From my brother in San Francisco, speaking about the downtown store that his wife works at: "The store was seriously vandalized with maybe one hundred or more looters. It is totally destroyed. Gut wrenching..."

From my sister in Big Bear: "A white friend posted, 'Why are *they* still protesting? The cops were arrested. This is time to find your inner peace, be calm, do silent protest, just sit. Justice will prevail.'" My sister responded to her friend, "There is no peace without justice."

From my sister in Escondido: "There have been a couple of times in my life that I fell to my knees to pray. The Hollister earthquake...and last night. While I was kneeling, I thought, why do we kneel at times like this? Then I thought, it grounds me. To be one with the floor or ground, calming my body, my nerves, then bowing my head to focus and pray."

From my sister in Sacramento: (After enduring the sounds of protestors and police that kept her awake, the next day my sister and her husband stopped to watch a large herd of goats cross a field at dusk.)

Sister: "That one has a black head and white body, that one is white, that one is spotted, that one is beige."

My brother-in-law, who is black, responded: "Goats of all colors are moving in unity toward the sun."

An athlete takes a knee to protest systemic racism, while a white cop knees out a black man's last breath. My sister falls to her knees to find the ground after the dominoes have all fallen and there is nothing left standing upright. The black son of an Atlanta cop tells us, "I woke up wanting to see the world burn down because I am tired (of racism) …". But then he adds, "Don't burn your own house down in anger at the enemy."

What is going on in our psyches with all this turmoil? I want to switch and look at how anger works in the brain and body. Here is an example of my behavior. One time I was angry while doing the dishes. I impulsively took the mug that was in my right hand, flung it down, and watched it smash into one hundred pieces against the tile kitchen floor. It felt so good for a second, but only for a second. My action left a permanent dent in the floor.

What is going on within us to make us react so impulsively when we are angry? We are all born with an instinct to react before thinking, which is called neuroception. This instinct is a survival tool. If we come across what looks like a rattlesnake on the road, we don't have time to wonder if we are in danger. We need to bypass thinking and go right for lifesaving action, like running away or fighting. When enraged, our bodies are energized instinctively to move toward action, as in protesting, yelling, hitting, throwing, or smashing something. We might break something small, like our favorite mug. Or we might destroy something big, like our own city. When the danger (perceived or real) is over, we settle down; our psyches readjust as our thinking brain comes back online.

Betrayal is the worst injury because it hurts a heart that had trust. In recent police violence against black citizens, the contract that the police equally protect and serve all citizens has been illuminated as false. In this case, long-simmering contained anger at racism was unleashed after the horrendous murder of George Floyd and others at the hands of the police. So, this country may need to endure a few days of mass violence, as some people who feel betrayed explode in outrage. Then people might calm down and channel that outrage into more productive ways to try and change a broken system. We can kneel in prayer and kneel in protest; then, we need to all stand up and move, but we need to move together toward justice. I hope that we can become like "the goats of all colors moving in unity toward the sun".

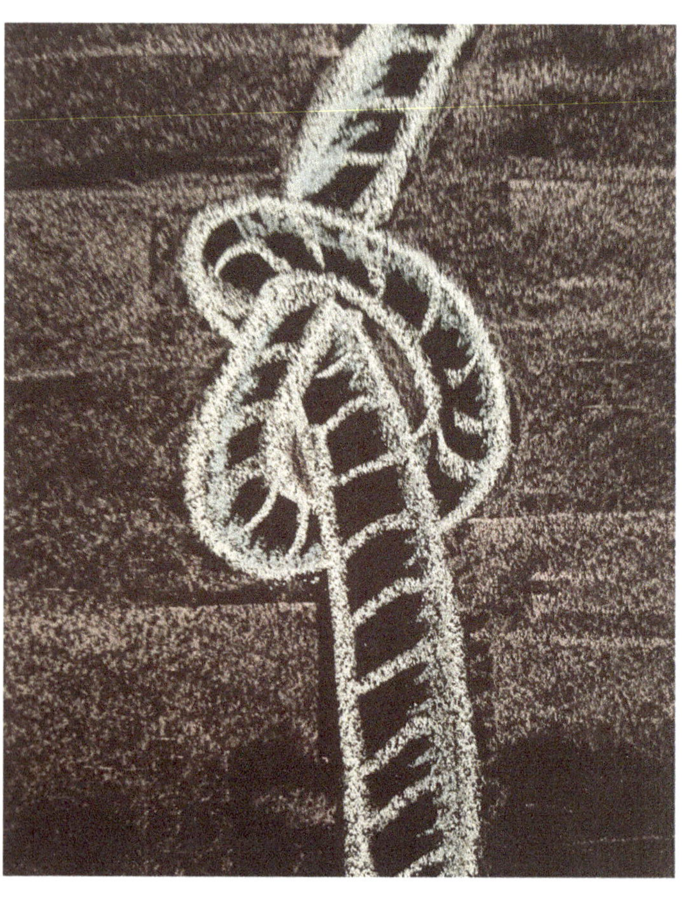

Knots

June 26, 2020:
Month four of pandemic

By the end of June, five hundred thousand people had died from the Coronavirus worldwide. Some countries eased restrictions to allow for summer business and social activities. In the USA, the issue of systemic racism rose to the front and took much of our attention. I felt compelled to become more informed.

Over eggs and toast at the dining room table, my husband and I compared where we were in the autobiographies we were separately reading. These were books from two prominent black men born in the 1920s in the USA. I was reading *The Fire Next Time* by James Baldwin, and he was reading *The Autobiography of Malcolm X.*

ME: As a young man James Baldwin saw there were two choices for him growing up in Harlem: joining a world of crime or joining a world of church. He became a young Christian minister.

HIM: Well, Malcolm X was raised with the same options, went into crime, met Elijah Mohammed, then went from a world of crime to a world of church, The Nation of Islam.

ME: Baldwin eventually realized he was being used in a power game, became disillusioned, and left the church. When Baldwin met Elijah Muhammed, he understood his appeal but was not drawn into his orbit.

HIM: Malcolm X's rising power in the Nation of Islam was a threat to its leader, Elijah Muhammed. In all likelihood, Muhammed had him assassinated.

As two white people, we are striving to broaden our view by listening to the voices of black lives. I know that I have a lot to learn to become more aware and become more involved in anti-racism effectively.

As a somatic psychotherapist, I am interested in how trauma affects the body. A colleague shared an interview with Resmaa Menakem, a clinical trauma therapist. When he was young, Resmaa was massaging the chubby hand of his petite grandmother and asked her, "Why are your hands fat, Grandma?" She said, "Picking cotton." It was in the weary and constricted tone of her voice that he could feel the trauma that she had lived. His book is called *My Grandmother's Hands: Racialized Trauma and the Pathway to Mending Our Hearts and Bodies.*

Menakem talks about the ways we hold our own race and the ways we see others. For example, he writes, "Black body sees white body as privileged, controlling and dangerous…Police bodies see black bodies as often dangerous or disruptive, as well as superhumanly powerful and impervious to pain. Our nervous systems are in knots." When I read that sentence, it hit home, and Menakem got me wondering about walking around with all this body tension.

What can we do to address walking around in knots?

One solution is to return to the body. This may include uncovering intergenerational trauma. If you are born to people already braced (like Menakem's grandmother), you pick up this lockdown in your psoas muscle. The psoas is a long deep muscle that originates in the lower back and extends through the pelvis to the front of the leg. If you feel a punch coming toward your stomach, you clench your belly, flex your hip and slightly lift your upper leg to protect your body. All these motions tighten and shorten the psoas muscle.

With chronic trauma, it is like always walking around with this clenched gut. Your body thinks it needs to stay permanently clenched to brace against seen or unseen danger. But in your brain, this bracing is often decontextualized and unconscious. So, you are tight but do not know it. This is what is called a "trauma pose". The trouble with staying braced in this pose is that it takes lots of effort and can diminish your joy in life. When the psoas muscle releases and we work through trauma, we take up more space to enjoy our life rather than be on alert all the time.

Here is a somatic practice that Menakem shares to "discover what lands and what is still in the air". I invite you to try this just to see what you notice.

Sit and orient to the room (this makes you look outward and around, which can interrupt a trauma pose of clenching and waiting for danger).

Look straight ahead. Register what you see.

Next, twist, look over your left shoulder, turn your hip (this engages the neck and stretches the psoas).

Notice what you experience. Return to center.

Look over your right shoulder. Turn your hip.

Notice what you experience. Return to center. Register what you notice in your body.

I have done this practice several times. This one time, I noticed various feelings that popped up. I felt cocky, and then I felt fragile, then I began to worry about some teens I know: the rich white ones, the poor white ones, the black ones.

Then I remembered a recent conversation I had with a young black male. I noticed his eyes veiled and almost shut, his head tilted down, and I asked him why he walked in this manner. He said, "I walk with my head down and don't open my eyes in public." He said this makes him feel safer out in the world. Although the young man knows he needs to be diligent in public, he stated that he is interested in reclaiming more of his joy in life through somatic psychotherapy.

Menakem uses an image to support somatic healing. "Like when you pick a car, then go buy it, then notice them on the road, and you never noticed them before. That is the promise of following your body, with its signs of trauma, signals of safety and danger. Once you pause and pay attention, you can bring your fears, rage, familial traumas to consciousness, and then begin to heal."

We may heal our bodies from walking around in a constant psoas tightened trauma pose, but we still need to address causes that come from the larger society. I am trying to open my eyes and learn more about the traumatic impact of racial injustice in America. To feel into the body of someone who, when he walks out the door, bows his head and tightens his gut for fear of mistreatment. I am looking at my own racism and fragility around white privilege. I want to learn how to be anti-racist. So far, I have tripped over a few rocks on that path and scraped my knees. But I need to keep going and tolerate some missteps by staying on the rocky path. I need to look beyond what usually lies right in front of my eyes, turn my head to the side, and head up the unfamiliar hill. This country is embroiled in division and it is time to follow our own bodies, not with comfortable strategies on familiar trails but by going inward and wrestling with the demons we carry in our souls and guts.

Anchor

September 2020:
Month seven of pandemic

In California, where I live, some people who had sheltered at home were forced to evacuate due to August wildfires. By September, there had been over thirty-two million COVID-19 cases and close to one million deaths in the world. Two hundred thousand of these deaths occurred in the USA. The presidential election was heating up, and there was a warning of the third surge in COVID cases expected from October through December 2020.

With all of this on my mind, I decided to take a walk with my small terrier. Heading back home from our evening stroll, a bulldog bolted from an open garage door and lunged at my dog with bared teeth. I pulled my dog's leash, but my dog wanted to fight, and I couldn't get him away. My eyes filled with terror as I imagined the larger dog snapping my dog's neck.

I felt desperate to break up this fight, and I knew I did not have much time. I yanked my dog up with all my might; my feet got knocked out from under me, and I fell onto the sidewalk. The neighbor ran out and grabbed her dog while I screamed for my husband, who got our dog and took him inside. The neighbor told her husband to take their dog in, and they both apologized profusely.

With my heart racing, I took a moment to check my body. My hands and elbow were scraped; my back felt okay. My neighbor wrung her hands. "Are you okay, are you okay?" I responded, "I think so."

My husband pulled me to my feet, and I went inside to check on our dog. No blood and no apparent injuries. I petted his red and cream coat and felt the warmth of his body. Still alive. My love for him brought tears to my eyes. How close to death and how quickly it could happen. My body shivered.

I moved to sit on the couch to gather myself. Anxiety made my heart speed and my gut tighten, while my eyes stayed big as saucers, even though the danger was gone. I looked at my watch. It was bedtime and I knew I was too distressed to sleep.

If you feel too stressed to sleep sometimes, here is a guided meditation from Oren Sofer, who teaches Mindfulness Meditation and Non-Violent Communication for Insight Meditation Society.

I asked my husband to find a guided meditation on anxiety. We settled in bed, and I heard the voice of the meditation leader Oren Sofer inviting me to return to the breath as "an anchor" as we explored anxiety. He gently asked us to become aware of the anxiety "story". "Is it a future worry? Is it a past remembrance?" (Yes, my dog was just attacked). "Now, put the story to the side and anchor in your body, return to the breath." The knots in my stomach loosened as I breathed and relaxed.

I heard Oren say, "Do not fight nor feed the anxiety." This made me feel a relaxed acceptance of my current state of being anxious without revving up into feeling more anxious. I followed the rest of the directions as I heard, "Where is it in the body?...Breathe into the lower body to reduce your anxiety… Loosen your jaw…"

In summary, the steps of this tool are:

1. Relax your body and bring your attention to your breath.

2. Use the breath as an anchor. Return to the breath whenever your anxiety rises.

3. Become aware of the anxiety story. Is it a future worry? Is it a past remembrance?

4. Put the story aside and return your focus to the breath.

5. Do not feed or fight the anxiety as it arises.

6. Ask, where is the anxiety located in my body?

7. Breathe into each body area that feels tense.

8. Slow your breath and allow waves of anxiety to be met with acceptance.

9. Return to the anchor of the breath until you feel more relaxed.

When I do this practice, I often add one more step. Here is how I processed the bulldog incident. I followed the guidelines but I added more, as my body surfed waves of different emotions that arose and fell. As a somatic psychotherapist, I believe in allowing the body to discharge strong emotional feelings. So, at the beginning of the meditation, I let myself cry to loosen the tension; then, I let my body shake out the fear, and my left fist began to tighten into a ball. I imagined socking that bulldog in the face and knocking him back. I took my hand and made punching gestures. My body relaxed after having discharged some of the pent-up tension from those feelings.

I turned on my side and pulled the covers over my shoulder to sleep after the meditation. My mind went to this: RBG (Ruth Bader Ginsburg, the eminent Supreme Court Justice) died today. What if my dog had died the same day as RBG? I sat up and reached out for my dog, who was curled at the foot of the bed. I petted his warm coat to make sure he was really still here. As my head sunk into the pillow and I drifted off to sleep, I saw them together from behind. She wore her long black robe and white pearl collar as she smiled down at my little red dog, who wagged his tail as they climbed a hill toward the clouds.

Rainbow

September 2020

The hardest part of 2020 for me was not seeing my daughter and her family in person. I live in California. They live in Missouri. And so we did video chats. The thirteen-year-old Zoomed with Papa to get eighth-grade math help, and the four-year-old took me by phone on video chat down into the basement and propped the phone up so we could play dinosaurs and playdoh together. The parents would flit in and out like birds to check in on us. But it was not the same. I missed the spontaneity of being with him in person, of squeezing his skin and running after him for hide and seek, watching him laugh and cuddling. The last time we "visited" by video chat, he put "me" on the couch when he got tired so we could watch Paw Patrol together.

My daughter called me on the way to pick up my four-year-old grandson after the first day of Fall at his pre-school. She told me he had graduated to the Rainbow Room. I can see him sitting in his car seat in the back of Mom's car while she drives.

"Nana, I'm in the big kids' class now!"
"That is great."
"Lots of new people. Lots of new toys."
"Was it fun?"
"Rowen was wearing crazy pants."
"Rowen is your best friend?"
"Yes. Hey, Nana, wanna go with me and see my school?"
"Ah, I would love to, but I can't."
"Tell Papa you wanna go with me."
(His mom interrupts): "Nana lives far away. She has to take a plane to get here."
"Get on a plane, Nana."
"I wish I could."
(His mom again): "As soon as people stop getting sick, Nana can travel to see us."
"I went two poo poos in the potty today, Mom."

I feel sad that it isn't safe enough to get on a plane to visit my little buddy or his older brother, whose voice has gone from tenor to baritone since I saw him last Christmas. I am missing their growth stages, and my heart hurts. My heart feels like a snail pulled from his shell.

If I could fly to you
Across the rainbow sky
I'd scoop you up and twirl you around
Way up high.

If I could fly to you
Across the rainbow sky

My tears would change from sad to glad
With happiness I'd cry.

If I could fly to you
Across the rainbow sky
I'd see your face, my pot of gold
And never say goodbye.

No Zen Grief

September 2020

As we all continued to witness so much grief, it brought me back to one of my most significant moments of suffering: the day when my mother would have turned one hundred if she were still alive.

As an artist, drawing often helps me express my emotions, but I could not draw on that day. I was sunk in sadness. The day that would have been my Mom's one-hundredth birthday hit me hard. She had died twelve years earlier. I had been working on a *Wizard of Oz* puzzle just to do something. I hoped that maybe if I finished the puzzle border, I would feel a little more chipper. It was not happening. So, I took a walk.

In the past week, nature had sung with brilliant lights and darks; now it looked just as draggy as I felt. I stared into the canyon. Trees and bushes were so still. Forced just to stand there, the trees were rooted in one place, unable to move. Then the wind blew, and some soggy leaves had to move like they were being pushed around against their will. On my walk, I wished only for that day to be over.

The only cheerful moment was when a neighbor's dog, also out for a walk that day, "wants to say hello," said the owner. I have seen my neighbor and her dog for years, and we had never interacted before that solemn day. I like to think Bridget (I asked and that was the dog's name) sensed my mood and wanted to comfort me.

After my attempt at cheering myself up by walking, I plopped onto the couch and scrolled through my phone messages. I was hoping to lighten the heavy load I was carrying by sharing it with others. I scrolled through posts from my siblings, who also felt burdened by grief that day. Some honored our mother by wearing her favorite black and red colors, wearing her earrings, or sending pictures of yellow roses, Mom's favorite. Then my brother Sean's text, "I miss my Mama" made me cry. Two other siblings said they felt melancholy too, and I made a few calls to get comfort and to give comfort.

After I hung up the phone, I had a realization: all of that sharing cut my pain in half. It was like I had been wading in molasses all day, and now the syrup was thinning, and I could move with greater ease. Later, I was touched by photos of three of my brothers who had taken flowers to the cemetery. By evening, sweet photos emerged of other siblings and grandkids eating lemon meringue pie, Mom's favorite dessert.

I remembered how we siblings cried in each other's arms at Mom's funeral. At the time, I wrote a poem about how our grief's similarity was the only thing that saved me. Kept me on the planet. What actions might help when overwhelming feelings of grief come to the surface?

1. Acknowledge your grief and notice how it feels in your body.

2. Be kind and do what you think might help (like walk, share your grief, soak up comfort from others).

What lessons might be taken from my mother's wisdom? My mother used to say, "Don't eat your bed", which was passed on from generations before. It was a warning to look for signs of indulging for too long in grief or depression. She believed that you should get up and get out of bed. Do something: move your body, work, play, take care of someone else, or do something creative.

The other message she used to say was, "This too shall pass." This is meant to encourage you to hold on until later, as your mood may lift with the passage of time.

The pandemic has increased grief across the world. Sometimes it hurts too much to be present in all this pain. However, it is important to acknowledge your suffering and be kind to yourself. You may need a day or two to pull into yourself and stay low. In addition, these two messages I learned from my mother may also be an aid to you in times of sorrow. When feeling very low, do not stay stuck in bed. Get up and move your body, if possible. Movement increases blood flow, which can improve your mood, at least a little. And when you are hovering dangerously low and want the ground to swallow you up, "a little" can go a long way. My Mom's other favorite, "this too shall pass", can be a glimpse of hope in the middle of an emotional or physical pain that seems like it will last forever. Thanks for these gifts, Mom.

Purple Reign

October 10, 2020:
Month eight of pandemic

"My son went to in-person school for one day; then, the county issued a purple alert and school was closed again. We are now back to having him do his first year of high school from home." This mother was lamenting the stress of dealing with changes due to the rise in COVID cases in her county.

"Purple Tier" refers to a Level 4 alert. The term was used for the highest risk factor for Coronavirus danger. It indicated a severe exposure and spread and asked that people only leave home for essential supplies and services. These alerts were a new system applied to slow the spread of the virus, which was in its third wave of rising. This wave was expected to continue through the end of 2020.

The color purple was also being used about current political trends. "My state of Arizona used to vote red but turned blue for Biden, so now we are a purple state." This indigenous woman joined other young voters as they rode two hours on horseback to vote in the United States presidential election of 2020.

A purple state refers to a swing or "battleground" state, where both Republican and Democratic candidates receive strong support without an overwhelming majority.

I looked out my second-floor window and saw the "Trump 2020" banner on the wall inside the open garage of my neighbor's house. The house across from it was flying what looked like an American flag but said, "Pro-America, Anti-Trump". These same people have kids who cross the street into each other's yards and play together during the day. The parents pass each other in the evening when they push strollers and walk their dogs in the cul de sac. But they do not talk about politics. Tension from political differences rose as the election date, November 3rd, grew closer.

I know a family who canceled their weekly Zoom visit because a few were blue Democrats, and most were red Republicans, and the fighting over politics turned to name-calling, anger and hurt. This hardening into ideological camps divided families. Each camp followed only one information channel.

I looked at a photo of my cousin when he was a kid. He looked so cute and innocent. But he had different views than I did about politics. I thought to myself, I can't believe he climbed on the "wrong" political train. It is almost like a feeling of betrayal because it is so hard to believe that he drank the Kool-Aid of distortion. Yet, my cousin probably felt the same way about me. Maybe this was a small taste of what the Civil War felt like when families took opposite sides, one fighting to preserve a way of life, the other to end slavery.

When there was as much division politically as there was in the USA in the autumn of 2020, people quickly saw evil intent on the other side. Conspiracy theories got people in a lather. Levels of fear and anger rose in a desperate attempt to either keep power or overthrow it. People screamed at each other until they turned blue (or red) in the face. No one seemed able to listen. Noisy and distant.

Take Christianity. The new "Patriot churches" were aligned with an authoritarian government and saw right-wing politics as the will of God. Another group called "Faithful America" fought to have Christianity seen as carrying Jesus's mantle for social justice. They were aligned with left-wing politics. These two camps took aim at each other and both claimed that God (as they understood Him) was on their side. In some way, both saw themselves as following Jesus. In the meantime, I pictured God looking down from heaven, shaking his head like Rodney King and saying, "Can't we all just get along?"

Once the presidential election ends, it will be time to braid red and blue threads together across the land. My mother used to braid my hair every morning before school. When I skipped, sometimes one braid flew behind me, while the other braid hit me in the face. Two braids with their own will. Like this country. I didn't have much hope for red and blue coming together but, once the election is over, I hope that the angry rhetoric will die down so people can walk down the street and smile at each other. It is time to accept reality and hope for compassion in humans to rise. It is also time to keep an eye on the sky, to attend to when purple clouds warn of a surge in COVID. It is time to heal.

I looked out the window. The five-year-old brown-haired boy crossed the lawn to the neighbor's house and asked the two blond sisters to ride bikes with him. Their voices rose in excitement as they strapped on helmets and disappeared down the road. Noisy and together.

Hike

October 11, 2020:
Month eight of pandemic

A kind of exhaustion blanketed the land. The ongoing pandemic had been unable to "flatten the curve" within this first year. Heightened political and economic strain caused millions of people to be out of work for months, and they felt desperate. Many "no-maskers" defied orders to wear a mask, which helps slow the spread of the virus. They saw it as an infringement of their rights to freedom. More people around us tested positive for the virus, and families could not attend their loved ones' funerals. We checked with our neighbor, who works for a testing company and keeps us abreast of vaccine development. She told us, "Vaccines are still in trials and not ready for the public." All this stress created a sense of fragility in some of us, as we could not feel much success in fighting the persistent storm.

Hiking is one activity that helps me shake off stress and feel better. On one trail, my feet in dusty hiking boots had to pay close attention to each uneven step on a rocky path up the mountain. After an hour of hiking this way, my heart felt over-stretched, like it was in a cage too small, so I leaned against the shady side of the hill and rested until I felt normal again. Then up I climbed. After ninety minutes, I sat to drink from my water bottle and let the autumn breeze cool my sweaty neck and arms. As my breathing evened out, I smelled sage, moist dirt, and lemonade berry.

After two hours of climbing, I saw, at my eye level, shiny black crows dip and turn, flying in broad circles in the sky. One flipped over, like swimming on his back, and then turned right side up again. It looked like he was playing with the wind. I sat to watch, as I had never seen crows like this. I usually frown at big crows when they dive for discarded food in the gutters where litter lines city streets. Out here, they looked happy.

All along the "Way Up Trail" were four-foot-tall metal markers topped with the shape of a quail. They marked hiking progress on the trail: 699 feet, 999 feet, then toward the peak: 1200 feet elevation.

At the peak, my husband and I took a road to picnic tables that overlooked a blue reservoir, cupped by the curved brown hills below us. After lunch, we took the trail back down. We saw a few people and most wore masks. They nodded and politely made way for each other on narrow parts of the path.

Traveling downhill was a breeze compared to climbing up. I smiled until I saw two dark-haired women right in the center of the path, blocking the way down. It was mid-afternoon and it looked like they were on the more difficult route up. One sat on a big rock. The other leaned over her. "Do you need help?" I asked as I got close. The middle-aged woman, who was standing, said, "Oh, no, we're fine." She looked embarrassed. The younger woman stood up slowly, and I looked at her. She was a teen whose eyes were red from crying. I was guessing her mother made her come, and she did not want to. She looked down. The mom said to us, "Well, there is a nice breeze." The daughter frowned and did not follow her mother up the trail. I looked at the teen and said, "I had to rest on the way up too. Just rest when you get tired. It's okay." The daughter nodded, offered a half-smile, stood up, turned, and trudged up the steep trail behind her mother.

As we headed down, we saw signs on the side that read, "Fragile Habitat, Please Stay on Trail". The signs were there because some people had taken shortcuts to avoid the longer way around, which had eroded the habitat.

I thought of a younger colleague who had called me recently. She ran her idea by me of a new way to look at working with clients in psychotherapy. She told me, "Using your 2009 paper, 'Borderline Revisited' as a jumping off point, I want to expand the idea that there are three levels of functioning within each personality type." I felt enthusiastic about her theory and encouraged her passion for writing a paper on the subject. Basically, she was advocating a new way to consider the level of fragility of each patient.

As we ended our hike and headed back to the car, I thought more about this idea of fragility. When you do not consider the level of fragility of the habitat (or person), you might take shortcuts that can cause damage. When the teen stopped in the middle of the path, she felt fragile at that moment. Her mom wanted her to look on the bright side and get moving. She stood still. I identified with her tiredness, to normalize resting on the path. That helped her be able to continue on the trail.

How do we shift "fragility" in people? I think we do it by understanding their level of need. We do it by joining in their world, by pausing, by resting, by taking stock of how our hearts, feet, noses, and whole bodies experience the world right now. I smelled sage and lemon and watched a happy crow fly upside down. The teen plopped down in the road and refused to move until someone said it was okay to rest. How do we save the fragile habitat in all of us? By listening to the body. That is the trail, that is the path we return to that leads us on.

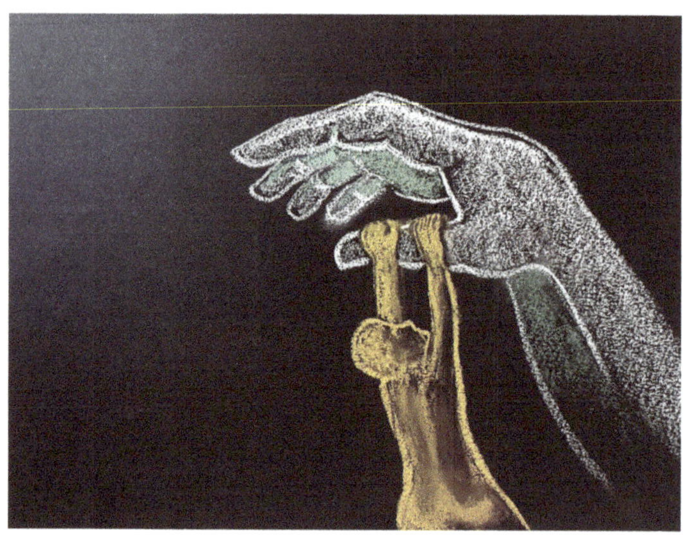

Brace Yourself

November 2020

One afternoon I was sitting on the couch, checking my messages, when I read, "…brace yourself because this isn't good news…" followed by a detailed note from my younger brother, letting us know that our oldest brother had just been diagnosed with prostate cancer. My oldest brother was like my father's right-hand man. He worked his whole childhood beside my father in our grocery store to help feed our large family. Although he loved sports, working after school kept him from becoming an athlete. Even though he could not participate himself, he often attended every track meet, baseball, basketball, and tennis game that some of us younger siblings played. We had more freedom to pursue some of our dreams because of how diligent and devoted our brother was.

Encouraging sentiments in the note like, "He is not suffering, and he likes his doctor" were interspersed with negative ones like, "He will have a bone scan next week to see if it has spread…the cancer is considered aggressive…" As I read this sad news, my head began to spin.

How do you cope with bad news and keep going?

Somewhere in my thinking brain, I did know the answer to that question. But that voice was small and faraway on the day I heard about my brother's cancer. That day I wrote in my journal, "I have entered the opium den of being spacey and in shock. I am aware of being in that state as I write this. I am writing this because I cannot do anything else. What was I doing right before the text from my brother? Working on edits for my book. I cannot focus on that now, which I resent a little because I have these timelines I set. But the gases of spaciness have poisoned the air, and my thinking brain cannot function well."

As soon as I had read the first line of the text, "brace yourself," I had stopped reading, left my desk to sit on the carpeted stairs, and pulled the dog near me. I knew I would need him as a body cushion to absorb the bad news. I understood that I had entered the part of my nervous system where shockiness is the body's defense against being overwhelmed. What happens is that if the news is so bad that we can't handle it in a clear-headed way, the brain will load us up with natural opiates so we can zone out and blunt the full force of pain. At least temporarily. So, as I floated in what felt like a semi-druggy state, I thanked my body for functioning to protect me.

I spoke to a few family members that day and then went for a walk around the neighborhood. I smiled at a teen neighbor washing his car, but I did not want to chat. Slowly pulling on an aromatic sprig of rosemary in the park, I remembered how all twelve of us siblings held hands at the front of the altar during my parent's fiftieth wedding anniversary Mass. That was twenty-five years ago. Both parents have since died and I realize our generation steps closer to the door of death. This is my oldest brother. He is in his early seventies. It is just the beginning of aging and illness and death eventually taking us all.

On the day that I heard about my brother's cancer diagnosis, I went to bed that night and had a dream of us siblings holding hands at that altar, and this time those hands separate. We reach in desperation, but our feet are planted and we can't reconnect our hands. I felt so distressed that I woke up and cried, taking in big gulps of air. I felt as if I was going down on a roller coaster at full speed. I know that the coaster will go back up again on the roller coaster of good and bad news. But on the day I heard about my brother's cancer, the roller coaster flew down at full speed, and all I could do was grip the bar and hold on.

All over the world people are getting calls to "brace yourself" as the pandemic continues to rage and take the health and often the lives of neighbors, friends and family members. Steadying ourselves on such shaky ground can be very difficult.

See if you can find a way to absorb the hit. Here are a few ways that might work.

1. While standing, slightly bend your knees up and down a few times and breathe deeply. This can make you feel more centered after a feeling of getting knocked over by emotional distress.

2. Sit down or lie down to feel your back supported and let your brain take you away by spacing out and going wherever it wants to go. This allows you to escape a while, which can help cushion the blow.

3. Cry if tears come and reach out and grab a hand if one is available.

Future

November 16, 2020:
Month nine of pandemic

We are into the ninth month of the pandemic, and it is clear that it will not end as 2020 comes to a close. In the beginning were unfounded promises that COVID-19 would not be serious, not last long, or not spread rapidly. All those promises to look to the future for a better tomorrow have not manifested. I found that the best strategy was to create my own routine and do the best I could to enjoy (as fully as I could) the present moment. I believe when we embrace the moment, we feel the most vibrant and alive. However, I did not always live up to that standard and one example was during a recent hike along the Rancho Carrillo Trail.

My gut felt tight as I walked fast on the trail. I thought I just wanted to get this exercise over with, so I could go back home and work on a project. I looked at my feet as my hiking boots crunched the graveled path. I inhaled and smelled the toyon tree. I saw that it was bursting with red holly berries. I exhaled. I caught up with my husband, Steve, to chat.

"Hey, I need an attitude adjustment."

"What do you mean?"

"My focus is on the future, like getting this hike over with. I need to focus on the present so that I can enjoy this hike."

"That's a good idea. I'll do that too."

After a half-hour on the fairly flat train, with the branches of green pepper trees bowing to gently lead us on our way, we came upon a sign. It said, "1.5 miles to Simmons Family Park. Level: Difficult." We had never gone along this particular path but nodded at each other and agreed to take this trail. The trail turned out to be all uphill. Sweat appeared on my neck, and I felt energized from the workout I was getting, especially for my thighs and hips. As we ascended the winding path, I looked to my right. The houses that had once been above us were now below us. Beyond them, I could see brown mountains and then the faint blue green of the ocean further west. I paused and inhaled, and the expansive view made me smile. As I took off hiking again, I noticed that my breathing was labored, and my thighs got more tired. In front of me was a sixty-five-degree angle straight up. I thought, well, it will be so lovely climbing back down. Oops. That was a future thought! I did not say this aloud due to my rule to stay in the present. I trudged up the hill.

I caught up with my husband (yes, he always goes faster than me), who was waiting at the top of that steep hill. He wiped his forehead and said, "It will be so nice going back down." We both laughed. We finally made it to this lush park that seemed like it was at the top of the world, with mowed green grass, a playground, and a pickleball court. We marveled at the spectacular 360-degree view of the world below. We sat on a bench in the shade to rest. The endorphins from good exercise made me happy, and I felt a smile spread over my face. My broad smile felt like a flower blooming. The endorphins also seemed to clear my head. As we walked down (and yes, it was much more pleasant going down than up), it hit me, and I talked with Steve about my new awareness.

"Do you know how I said I need to be in the present and not the future?"

"Yeah."

"Well, when my legs were sore, my mind went to the future."

"Mine too."

"I think when you are suffering, it is natural to think of a better future."

"Right, it gives you the hope to go on."

We scrambled down the hill, finding some loose dirt a little slippery, but it was mostly pleasant. I saw a shirtless young man with a red face coming uphill toward me. As he glanced up the hill with a worried look, I said, "You are almost there." I figured he needed a little hope for a less painful future.

Don't Give Up

November 30, 2020:
Final week of month nine of pandemic

In the last week of November, we had Thanksgiving dinner in our backyard with places set six feet apart for our three guests. My sister, who lives in the desert, wanted to walk on the beach the next day. Our experience reminded me that even though we have all felt wounded by this very challenging year, it is essential to do what we can to keep going.

As I walked on the beach with my sister, I turned and stopped to face the ultramarine water burst into white foam waves. The waves became smaller as they slid forward and bubbled over my bare feet when they reached the shore. As the waves receded, the hard ground beneath me softened, and my feet molded into a spongy texture. Then I heard a yelp.

I looked to my right. My sister and I saw two off-leash small dogs. One of the dogs attacked a seagull and seemed to be pulling at his wing. A man and a woman yelled and pulled their dog off the bird, leashed their dogs, and left the beach. The woman turned back to look at the gull, then her head shrunk into her shoulders, and she slouched away as fast as she could.

We watched the bird and worried about his plight. Would he be okay? He sat on the shore, looking stunned. I noticed eleven other gulls at a respectful distance, staring at him and not moving. They seemed to be waiting. The injured gull made a tentative step, then walked in a circle, but one wing was much lower and spread out and down. Was his shoulder broken?

The gull walked into the ocean and swam around slowly. His mates all turned and watched him. A lifeguard truck came by, and I went up to meet it. Seeing me coming, the lifeguard donned his face mask and rolled down his window so I could talk to him.

"A dog attacked a seagull."

"We have an animal control unit, but they don't work during the pandemic."

"Why are the other birds staring?"

"They stay in a flock. They hunt together by day and nest together at night."

"So, they are watching over him?"

"Yes."

My sister and I cheered on the injured bird. He swam around, then tried to fly and failed once or twice, as his wings did not synchronize. He stopped. The birds stared. We stared. I hoped he was resting rather than giving up.

After five minutes, he came ashore, all birds' eyes on him, got a running start, and took to the sky. He flew above and behind us. His wings were working! My sister and I yelled, "Whoo-hoo." As we turned toward the hills to follow the circling bird, I saw a woman in an orange sweatshirt yell, "Hurray, you go gull!"

I felt so happy and relieved. I exhaled, turned back to my sister and smiled. She stood tall, lifted her chin, and solemnly quoted this Langston Hughes poem[2] to me:

Hold fast to dreams
for if dreams die
life is a broken-winged bird
that cannot fly.

Hold fast to dreams
for if dreams go
life is a barren field
frozen with snow.

2   "Dreams" from *The Collected Poems of Langston Hughes* by Langston Hughes, edited by Arnold Rampersad with David Roessel, Associate Editor, copyright @ 1994 by the Estate of Langston Hughes. Used by permission of Alfred A. Knopf, an imprint of the Knopf Doubleday Publishing Group, a division of Penguin Random House LLC. All rights reserved.

Closing

As I write this closing in December 2020, a promising vaccine against COVID-19 has begun to be distributed worldwide. Our attention will most likely turn toward the availability of the vaccine and we will follow its effectiveness with fingers crossed in hope. I feel proud that we have this ray of sun breaking through a dark-clouded year. My closing message for you is to remember that no matter what happens in the outside world, even if it does not feel like it, you always have some control over your inside world.

In a year of turmoil, our stress rose as we tried to cope. Some coping skills work better than others, like breathing, grounding and reaching for help. And some do not work well at all, like self-hate, blaming and letting fear or hate overwhelm us so that we miss moments of grace and beauty.

I hope after reading these stories, you understand better how your brain works during stress and perhaps grab a few tools that help you feel more balanced.

My wish is that you continue to breathe into your body and find that spark that grounds you in your light.

My desire is that you walk away taking better care of yourself and like a daffodil that pokes its yellow head through the hard, frozen, winter ground, you embrace hope for a better tomorrow.

Acknowledgments

When I told my writing coach, Marni Freedman, that I had the idea of putting some of my blog posts into a small chapbook, she said, "Great idea." That is Marni. Not only enthusiastic but a knowledgeable content editor who expertly shepherds books on the road to becoming a decent, polished product. I should know as this is our third collaboration. I so appreciate your ongoing support of me, Marni. Tony Bonds, of Golden Ratio Book Design, took the helm and worked with me on the production side of this book. I admired his artistic eye and cheerful demeanor as he placed all the pieces in publishable form. Andrea Glass is my go-to copyeditor, who was such a great help, as she was on my previous book. Thanks to my husband, Steve, who generously gave me his opinion on every post. I want to thank my daughter, my grandkids and my family and friends for weaving your spells of love and connection through the fabric of my life.